YOUR COMPLETE VIRGO 2024 PERSONAL HOROSCOPE

Monthly Astrological Prediction Forecast Readings of Every Zodiac Astrology Sun Star Signs- Love, Romance, Money, Finances, Career, Health, Travel, Spirituality.

Iris Quinn

Alpha Zuriel Publishing

Copyright © 2023 by **Iris Quinn**

All rights reserved. No part of this publication may be reproduced, distributed or transmitted in any form or by any means, without prior written permission.

**Alpha Zuriel Publishing
United States.**

The content contained within this book may not be reproduced, duplicated or transmitted without direct written permission from the author or the publisher.
Under no circumstances will any blame or legal responsibility be held against the publisher, or author, for any damages, reparation, or monetary loss due to the information contained within this book; either directly or indirectly.

Legal Notice:
This book is copyright protected. This book is only for personal use. You cannot amend, distribute, sell, use, quote or paraphrase any part, or the content within this book, without the consent of the author or publisher.

Disclaimer Notice:
Please note the information contained within this document is for educational and entertainment purposes only. All effort has been executed to present accurate, up to date, and reliable, complete information. No warranties of any kind are declared or implied. Readers acknowledge that the author is not engaging in the rendering of legal, financial, medical or professional advice.

Your Complete Virgo 2024 Personal Horoscope/ Iris Quinn. -- 1st ed.

"In the dance of the planets, we find the rhythms of life. Astrology reminds us that we are all connected to the greater universe, and our actions have ripple effects throughout the cosmos."
— IRIS QUINN

CONTENTS

- VIRGO PROFILE 1
- PERSONALITY OF VIRGO 5
- WEAKNESSES OF VIRGO 7
- RELATIONSHIP COMPATIBILITY WITH VIRGO 10
- LOVE AND PASSION 18
- MARRIAGE 20
- VIRGO 2024 HOROSCOPE 23
  - Overview Virgo 2024 23
  - January 2024 29
  - February 2024 37
  - March 2024 42
  - April 2024 47
  - May 2024 52
  - June 2024 57
  - July 2024 62
  - August 2024 67
  - September 2024 72
  - October 2024 78
  - November 2024 84
  - December 2024 90

1 · COMPLETE VIRGO 2024 PERSONAL HOROSCOPE

CHAPTER ONE

VIRGO PROFILE

- Constellation: Virgo
- Zodiac Symbol: The Virgin
- Date: August 23 - September 22
- Element: Earth
- Ruling Planet: Mercury
- Career Planet: Saturn
- Love Planet: Venus
- Money Planet: Mercury
- Planet of Fun, Entertainment, Creativity, and Speculations: Sun
- Planet of Health and Work: Mercury
- Planet of Home and Family Life: Moon
- Planet of Spirituality: Neptune
- Planet of Travel, Education, Religion, and Philosophy: Jupiter

Colors:
- Colors: Navy Blue, Gray

- Colors that promote love, romance, and social harmony: Peach, Pastel Pink
- Color that promotes earning power: Emerald Green

- Gem: Sapphire
- Metals: Mercury, Nickel
- Scent: Lavender
- Birthstone: Sapphire

Qualities:
- Quality: Mutable (Adaptability)
- Quality most needed for balance: Spontaneity.

Strongest Virtues:
- Analytical Thinking
- Organizational Skills
- Attention to Detail
- Practicality
- Reliability

Deepest Need: Order and Stability

- Characteristics to Avoid:
- Excessive Criticism
- Overthinking
- Perfectionism

- Hyper-focus on Details

Signs of Greatest Overall Compatibility:
- Taurus
- Capricorn

Signs of Greatest Overall Incompatibility:
- Pisces
- Sagittarius

- Sign Most Supportive for Career Advancement: Capricorn
- Sign Most Supportive for Emotional Well-being: Cancer
- Sign Most Supportive Financially: Taurus
- Sign Best for Marriage and/or Partnerships: Libra
- Sign Most Supportive for Creative Projects: Leo
- Best Sign to Have Fun With: Taurus

Signs Most Supportive in Spiritual Matters:
- Scorpio
- Pisces

Best Day of the Week: Wednesday

VIRGO TRAITS

- Perfectionistic tendencies
- Detail-oriented
- Analytical thinkers
- Highly organized
- Practical and logical
- Critical of themselves and others
- Reserved and introverted

PERSONALITY OF VIRGO

The personality of a Virgo is characterized by a unique blend of traits that contribute to their overall nature. Virgos are known for their practicality, attention to detail, and analytical thinking. They have a natural inclination towards order and organization, and they excel at planning and problem-solving. Virgos are highly observant and possess a keen eye for even the smallest details. They are often perfectionistic and have high standards for themselves and others.

Virgos are dedicated and hardworking individuals who take their responsibilities seriously. They have a strong sense of duty and are committed to doing things to the best of their ability. With their analytical minds, Virgos are adept at analyzing situations and finding practical solutions. They possess excellent critical thinking skills and have a strong sense of logic.

While Virgos have a reputation for being reserved and introverted, they are also known for their kindness and helpful nature. They are reliable friends and are always willing to lend a hand when needed. Virgos have a nurturing side and take pleasure in supporting and assisting others.

On the downside, Virgos can be overly critical, both of themselves and those around them. They have a tendency to focus on flaws and imperfections, which can sometimes lead to excessive worry and self-doubt. Virgos may also struggle with expressing their emotions openly, preferring to keep their feelings more private.

Overall, the personality of a Virgo is characterized by practicality, attention to detail, dedication, and a strong sense of responsibility. They strive for perfection and possess excellent analytical skills, but they should be mindful of their tendency to be overly critical and self-critical.

WEAKNESSES OF VIRGO

Virgo, the meticulous perfectionist, bears within them a set of weaknesses that intertwine with their inherent traits. Their pursuit of excellence and attention to detail can often manifest as an overwhelming need for perfection, causing them to be excessively critical of themselves and others. This self-imposed pressure can lead to self-doubt and a constant feeling of falling short, hindering their ability to appreciate their accomplishments.

With their analytical minds constantly at work, Virgos have a propensity to overthink and scrutinize every aspect of their lives. This incessant analysis can create a sense of mental restlessness, as they tirelessly seek to find solutions and make sense of the world around them. This tendency to overanalyze can sometimes lead to a state of indecision, as they weigh every possible outcome and strive for the perfect course of action.

Virgos' meticulous nature also extends to their relationships, as they hold high standards for themselves and those around them. This can result in a critical outlook that may inadvertently strain their connections with others. They may find it challenging to embrace imperfections and allow for spontaneity and flexibility in their interactions.

In their pursuit of order and control, Virgos may exhibit a need for structure and routine that can sometimes stifle their sense of adventure and spontaneity. They may struggle to let go and embrace the unknown, preferring the comfort of the familiar and the predictable.

While Virgos' attention to detail can be a valuable asset, it can also manifest as nitpicking and excessive focus on minor flaws. This inclination to fixate on imperfections can create a sense of dissatisfaction and prevent them from fully appreciating the beauty and essence of the present moment.

Additionally, Virgos may harbor a tendency towards overworking themselves and neglecting their own well-being. Their relentless pursuit of perfection and their desire to fulfill their responsibilities can lead to burnout and a neglect of their physical and emotional needs.

It is important to note that these weaknesses are not inherent flaws, but rather aspects of the Virgo personality that can be addressed and balanced with self-awareness and self-care. By embracing self-compassion and cultivating a sense of acceptance, Virgos can harness their strengths while finding a healthier equilibrium in their pursuit of perfection.

RELATIONSHIP COMPATIBILITY WITH VIRGO

Based only on their Sun signs, this is how Virgo interacts with others. These are the compatibility interpretations for all 12 potential Virgo combinations. This is a limited and insufficient method of determining compatibility.

However, Sun-sign compatibility remains the foundation for overall harmony in a relationship.

The general rule is that yin and yang do not get along. Yin complements yin, and yang complements yang. While yin and yang partnerships can be successful, they require more effort. Earth and water zodiac signs are both Yin. Yang is represented by the fire and air zodiac signs.

Virgo and Aries (Yin/Yang)

Virgo and Aries bring different energies to a relationship, which can create a dynamic but challenging partnership. Virgo's practicality and attention to detail may clash with Aries' spontaneous and impulsive nature. Both signs have strong personalities and may need to work on understanding and appreciating each other's strengths. By finding a balance between structure and spontaneity, they can create a relationship that combines practicality with excitement.

Virgo and Taurus (Yin/Yin)

Virgo and Taurus share an Earth element, which provides a solid foundation for their relationship. Both signs value stability, loyalty, and security in a partnership. They can create a harmonious connection based on trust, dependability, and shared values. However, Virgo's analytical nature and perfectionist tendencies may clash with Taurus' stubbornness and resistance to change. By practicing patience, understanding, and open communication, they can navigate challenges and build a lasting bond.

Virgo and Gemini (Yin/Yang)

Virgo and Gemini bring different energies and communication styles to their relationship. Virgo's practicality and attention to detail may clash with

Gemini's desire for variety and intellectual stimulation. However, both signs possess intellectual curiosity and can engage in meaningful conversations. By embracing open communication, adaptability, and compromise, they can find a balance that respects both Virgo's need for structure and Gemini's need for freedom. With patience and understanding, they can create a relationship that values both stability and mental exploration.

Virgo and Cancer (Yin/Yin)

Virgo and Cancer share a mutual understanding and appreciation for emotional depth and security in a relationship. Both signs value loyalty, commitment, and nurturing. They can create a strong bond built on trust, support, and shared values. However, Virgo's analytical nature and critical tendencies may clash with Cancer's emotional sensitivity. By practicing empathy, patience, and open-hearted communication, they can navigate their differences and create a loving and supportive partnership.

Virgo and Leo (Yin/Yang)

Virgo and Leo have contrasting energies that can create both attraction and challenges in their relationship. Virgo's practicality and attention to detail may clash with Leo's desire for attention and grand gestures. Both signs have strong personalities and may need to work on understanding and appreciating each other's strengths. By embracing open communication, compromise, and finding ways to support and uplift each other, they can create a dynamic and fulfilling partnership that values both practicality and passion.

Virgo and Virgo (Yin/Yin)

When two Virgo individuals come together, their shared traits and values create a strong foundation for their relationship. Both Virgos are practical, analytical, and detail-oriented, which can create a harmonious partnership built on shared understanding and common goals. They appreciate organization, order, and efficiency in their lives, and can work together to create a structured and productive environment.

However, their perfectionist tendencies and critical nature may occasionally lead to conflicts or disagreements. Both Virgos need to be mindful of their tendency to overanalyze and nitpick, as it can create unnecessary tension.

Virgo and Libra (Yin/Yang)

Virgo and Libra bring different qualities to their relationship, creating a balance when approached with understanding and compromise. Virgo's practicality and analytical skills can complement Libra's charm and diplomacy. Both signs appreciate harmony and balance, but they may need to navigate Virgo's critical nature and Libra's indecisiveness. By practicing open communication, patience, and finding ways to meet in the middle, they can create a partnership that values both practicality and harmony.

Virgo and Scorpio (Yin/Yin)

Virgo and Scorpio share a deep connection based on mutual understanding and intensity. Both signs value loyalty, commitment, and depth in relationships. They can create a profound bond built on trust, emotional intimacy, and shared values. However, Virgo's analytical nature and perfectionist tendencies may clash with Scorpio's intense emotions and desire for control. By practicing open communication, trust, and respect for boundaries, they can navigate their differences and create a transformative and passionate partnership.

Virgo and Sagittarius (Yin/Yang)

Virgo and Sagittarius have different approaches to life, which can create both excitement and challenges in their relationship. Virgo's practicality and attention to detail may clash with Sagittarius' desire for adventure and freedom. Both signs have independent spirits and may need to work on understanding and respecting each other's need for stability and spontaneity. By embracing open-mindedness, compromise, and finding common interests, they can navigate their differences and create a relationship that embraces growth, exploration, and mutual support.

Virgo and Capricorn (Yin/Yin)

Virgo and Capricorn share a grounded and practical approach to life, forming a highly compatible partnership. Both signs value hard work, responsibility, and stability, and they can support each other in achieving their goals. They have a shared sense of duty and a strong work ethic, making them a power couple in both professional and personal endeavors. Their commitment to each other's success and their willingness to provide practical support creates a solid and long-lasting relationship.

Virgo and Aquarius (Yin/Yang)

Virgo and Aquarius have different approaches to life, but their unique qualities can complement each other in a relationship. Virgo's practicality and attention to detail can balance Aquarius' visionary and unconventional nature. They can inspire each other to broaden their perspectives and embrace new ideas. However, they may need to navigate differences in communication styles and adaptability. By fostering open-mindedness and finding common ground, they can create a dynamic and intellectually stimulating partnership.

Virgo and Pisces (Yin/Yang)

Virgo and Pisces have a contrasting yet complementary energy that can create a harmonious and balanced relationship. Virgo's practicality and attention to detail can provide grounding for Pisces' dreamy and imaginative nature. They can support each other in pursuing their goals and creating a harmonious home environment. However, they may need to work on understanding each other's emotional needs and finding ways to bridge the gap between their practicality and sensitivity. With patience, empathy, and open communication, they can build a deep and supportive connection.

LOVE AND PASSION

Virgos approach love with a rational and analytical mindset. They value stability, trust, and loyalty in their relationships. When it comes to passion, Virgos may not be the most overtly expressive, but their love runs deep and is often expressed through acts of service and dedication.

Virgos are attentive partners who strive to meet their loved one's needs and create a harmonious environment. They take their time to understand their partner's desires and make an effort to fulfill them. Their attention to detail ensures that they remember the little things that matter, making their partners feel cherished and loved.

In intimate moments, Virgos bring their meticulous nature into play. They pay careful attention to their partner's desires and take pleasure in creating a comfortable and sensual experience. Their sensuality is often understated but deeply felt. They value the physical and emotional connection with their partner, seeking a sense of intimacy that goes beyond the surface level.

While Virgos may not be inclined towards grand gestures or extravagant displays of passion, their love is consistent and enduring. They prioritize the long-term aspects of a relationship, striving for emotional security and mutual growth. Virgos appreciate open and honest communication, and they value intellectual compatibility and shared values in their romantic connections.

However, Virgos may also have a tendency to overanalyze and worry, which can sometimes lead to self-doubt and caution in matters of the heart. They may take time to fully open up and trust their partner, as they want to ensure a solid foundation before diving into deep emotional waters.

Overall, love and passion for Virgos are expressed through practicality, devotion, and a commitment to building a stable and fulfilling relationship. Their genuine care, loyalty, and attention to detail create a foundation for lasting love, where both partners feel valued, supported, and cherished.

MARRIAGE

Virgos approach marriage with a practical and responsible mindset. They value stability, loyalty, and commitment, and they are generally supportive of the institution of marriage. However, before taking the leap, Virgos tend to prioritize their financial stability and security, ensuring that they have a solid foundation to build their married life upon.

In a marriage, Virgos bring their meticulous nature and attention to detail into play. They have a strong desire for order, efficiency, and organization, and they strive to create a harmonious and well-structured home environment. Virgo women, in particular, excel at balancing their work and family duties, ensuring that both aspects of their life receive equal attention and dedication.

While Virgos may be highly committed to their marriage, they need to be mindful of their tendency to be critical and perfectionistic. They have high standards for themselves and their partner, which can sometimes lead to nitpicking and disputes. It is important for Virgos to learn to communicate their concerns and expectations in a constructive manner, fostering open dialogue and understanding within the marriage.

Virgo men, on the other hand, are dedicated and responsible husbands and fathers. They value equality and fairness in their relationships, ensuring that their spouse does not carry an unequal burden of responsibilities. They actively participate in household tasks and parenting, contributing their fair share to create a balanced and supportive partnership.

While Virgos may strive to keep their marriage alive and strong, they are not afraid to acknowledge when disagreements become insurmountable. They are practical individuals who understand the importance of their own well-being and happiness. If they feel that the relationship is no longer serving their emotional or personal growth, they may choose to end the marriage, seeking a healthier and more fulfilling path.

Overall, marriage for Virgos is characterized by dedication, practicality, and a strong desire for order and stability. They bring their analytical and responsible nature into their marital roles, ensuring that their partnership is well-structured and balanced. With open communication, understanding, and a willingness to work through challenges, Virgos can create a lasting and fulfilling marriage where both partners feel supported, respected, and valued.

CHAPTER TWO

VIRGO 2024 HOROSCOPE

Overview Virgo 2024

As we step into the year 2024, Virgo, the celestial bodies have a unique narrative to weave for you. This year will be a time of growth, change, and opportunities. The planetary movements indicate a year filled with potential and challenges that will help you evolve and grow. The universe is aligning in a way that will push you to explore new horizons, delve deeper into your passions, and embrace the essence of who you are.

The year 2024 will be a significant one for your career, Virgo. The alignment of Mars and Jupiter in Gemini in June suggests a time of increased activity and opportunities in your professional life. This could manifest in various ways - perhaps a promotion is on the horizon, or a new job offer that aligns more with your passions. You may find yourself taking on new responsibilities or embarking on new projects. This is a time to step out of your comfort zone and seize these opportunities.

Financially, the trine between Mercury in Cancer and Saturn in Pisces in late June indicates stability. You may find that your financial situation is solidifying, and this could be a good time to save or invest. This is a year to make wise financial decisions - consider seeking advice from a financial advisor or doing thorough research before making significant financial moves.

In the realm of relationships, Venus's movement into Cancer in mid-June suggests a time of emotional depth and connection. You may find yourself feeling more in tune with your loved ones and forming deeper bonds. This is a time to nurture your relationships - spend quality time with your loved ones, express your feelings openly, and strengthen your connections.

However, be mindful of Venus's square with the True Node in Aries later in the month, which may bring challenges or conflicts. These conflicts may test your patience and understanding, but remember, they are also opportunities for growth. Approach these situations with empathy and open communication.

In terms of your social life, this year will bring opportunities to expand your social circle. You may find yourself meeting new people and forming new friendships. Embrace these opportunities and enjoy the richness that diverse relationships can bring to your life.

Your health and wellness are highlighted in 2024, particularly in August, with Venus moving into Virgo. This is a time to focus on self-care and nurturing your physical well-being. Consider incorporating a new fitness routine into your schedule, or perhaps try a new healthy diet. This is also a time to pay attention to your mental health - consider practices like meditation or yoga to maintain a balanced state of mind.

However, the square between Venus and Uranus in Taurus suggests potential stress or upheaval. Be sure to balance your time and energy and take care of your mental health as well. Remember, it's okay to take a break and rest when needed. Your health and well-being should always come first.

Spiritually, 2024 is a year of growth and development. The sesquiquadrate between Jupiter in

Gemini and Pluto in Aquarius in August suggests a time of deep transformation. This is a year to explore your spiritual beliefs and practices, and you may find yourself drawn to new philosophies or ways of thinking. Consider exploring different spiritual practices - perhaps try meditation, or delve into the world of mindfulness.

The Sun's sextile with Jupiter in Gemini in August also indicates a time of personal expansion and learning. This is a time to embrace personal development - consider taking up a new hobby, learning a new skill, or perhaps embarking on a journey of self-discovery.

In conclusion, Virgo, 2024 is a year of opportunities, challenges, and growth. From career advancements to deepening relationships, to personal and spiritual development, the stars align to provide a year of significant evolution. Embrace the journey, and remember, every challenge is an opportunity for growth.

This year, you will be called to step out of your comfort zone and embrace change. You will be asked to delve deeper into your relationships, to nurture your health and well-being, and to explore your spiritual side. You will be given opportunities to grow, to learn, and to evolve.

In your career, be open to new opportunities and challenges. They will push you to grow and evolve in ways you may not have anticipated. In your relationships, be open to deepening connections and resolving conflicts. They will teach you about love, patience, and understanding. In your health and wellness, remember to take care of yourself. Your physical and mental well-being is crucial to your overall happiness and success.

In your spiritual growth and personal development, be open to new ideas and practices. They will help you understand yourself and the world around you on a deeper level.

2024 is a year of growth, change, and evolution. It's a year to embrace who you are and who you are becoming. So, Virgo, step into this year with an open heart and an open mind. Embrace the journey and the growth that comes with it. Remember, the stars are on your side, guiding you and supporting you every step of the way.

As we conclude, remember that these are general trends and individual experiences may vary. Always listen to your intuition and make decisions that are right for you. Here's to a transformative and enriching 2024, Virgo!

January 2024

Horoscope

January 2024 brings a mix of planetary aspects that will have a significant impact on the Virgo individuals. The month begins with a square aspect between Venus in Sagittarius and Saturn in Pisces on January 1st, which may create some tension in your relationships. It's important to communicate openly and honestly to avoid misunderstandings and conflicts. On January 3rd, Venus forms a quincunx aspect with Jupiter, which could bring some challenges in matters of love and romance. It's advisable to find a balance between your desires and the expectations of your partner.

Mercury forms a quintile aspect with Saturn on the same day, offering you mental clarity and the ability to make practical decisions. This alignment supports your communication skills and helps you express your thoughts effectively. Additionally, on January 3rd, Mars forms a semi-sextile aspect with Pluto, indicating a need for balance and self-control in dealing with power dynamics and conflicts.

The Sun forms a quintile aspect with Neptune on January 3rd, enhancing your intuition and spiritual awareness. This is an excellent time for self-reflection and exploring your inner world. However, on January 6th, the Sun squares Chiron, which may bring up some emotional wounds or insecurities. Take this opportunity to heal and grow from past experiences.

Your ruling planet, Mercury, forms a trine with Jupiter on January 19th, boosting your intellectual abilities and expanding your knowledge. This is a favorable time for learning, studying, or pursuing new ventures. However, be mindful of Venus square Neptune on the same day, which may create some illusions or unrealistic expectations in relationships. Take things slowly and ensure that your romantic endeavors are based on a solid foundation.

As the month progresses, the Sun conjuncts Pluto on January 20th, bringing intensity and transformation to your life. This alignment may lead to profound inner changes and empower you to let go of what no longer serves you.

Overall, January 2024 is a month of growth and self-reflection for Virgo individuals. It's essential to maintain open communication in relationships, be cautious of unrealistic expectations, and embrace the opportunities for personal and professional development.

Love

In January 2024, Virgo individuals will experience a mixed bag of influences in matters of love and romance. The square aspect between Venus in Sagittarius and Saturn in Pisces on January 1st may create some challenges and tension in your relationships. It's crucial to maintain open and honest communication to navigate through any misunderstandings or conflicts that may arise during this time.

On January 3rd, Venus forms a quincunx aspect with Jupiter, which could lead to some adjustments and compromises in your love life. It's important to find a balance between your personal desires and the expectations of your partner. Avoid making impulsive decisions and take the time to understand each other's needs and perspectives.

However, on January 8th, Venus forms a harmonious biquintile aspect with Jupiter, bringing a period of joy, growth, and abundance in your relationships. This alignment enhances your love life, allowing for deeper emotional connections and increased harmony. It's an excellent time to express your affection and strengthen the bond with your partner.

Throughout the month, be cautious of Venus square Neptune on January 19th, which may create illusions or unrealistic expectations in your romantic endeavors. It's essential to approach relationships with clarity and discernment, ensuring that your connections are based on mutual trust and understanding.

Career

January 2024 presents both challenges and opportunities in your professional life, Virgo. The month begins with a square aspect between Venus in Sagittarius and Saturn in Pisces on January 1st. This alignment may bring some obstacles or delays in your career endeavors. Patience and persistence are key during this period. Focus on refining your skills, improving your work ethic, and maintaining a positive attitude.

On January 19th, Mercury forms a trine with Jupiter, bringing favorable influences for career advancement and intellectual growth. This alignment enhances your communication skills, making it an excellent time for negotiations, presentations, or networking. Embrace opportunities for learning and expanding your knowledge, as they may lead to professional success.

However, be cautious of Venus square Neptune on the same day, as it may bring some confusion or unrealistic expectations in your professional relationships. Ensure that you have a clear understanding of your goals and stay grounded in your aspirations.

Finance

January 2024 presents a mixed bag of influences when it comes to your finances, Virgo. The square aspect between Venus in Sagittarius and Saturn in Pisces on January 1st may create some financial constraints or delays. It's essential to adopt a practical and disciplined approach to your finances during this time. Budgeting, saving, and avoiding impulsive purchases will help you maintain stability.

On January 8th, Venus forms a biquintile aspect with Jupiter, indicating a favorable time for financial growth and abundance. This alignment may bring unexpected opportunities or windfalls. However, be cautious of overspending or taking unnecessary risks. It's important to maintain a balanced approach and make informed decisions.

Health

In January 2024, it's crucial for Virgo individuals to prioritize their health and well-being. The month begins with a square aspect between Venus in Sagittarius and Saturn in Pisces on January 1st. This alignment may bring some emotional or physical strain. Take time for self-care, engage in activities that bring you joy, and seek support from loved ones.

On January 6th, the Sun squares Chiron, which may trigger some emotional wounds or insecurities. Focus on healing and self-compassion during this time. Engaging in therapy, meditation, or other healing practices can be beneficial.

The Sun's trine with Uranus on January 9th brings a surge of energy and opportunities for positive changes in your well-being. Embrace new exercise routines, dietary improvements, or holistic approaches to maintain a healthy lifestyle.

Throughout the month, ensure you listen to your body's needs and practice self-care regularly. By maintaining a balanced approach to your physical and emotional well-being, you can navigate January with resilience and vitality.

Travel

January 2024 may offer some opportunities for travel, exploration, and adventure for Virgo individuals. However, it's important to consider the prevailing planetary aspects to make the most of your journeys.

On January 8th, Venus forms a biquintile aspect with Jupiter, enhancing your enthusiasm for new experiences and connections. This alignment supports positive interactions during your travels and brings opportunities for personal growth.

Additionally, on January 22nd, Mars forms a quintile aspect with Neptune, infusing your journeys with creativity, inspiration, and a sense of adventure. It's a great time to explore new destinations or engage in activities that allow you to tap into your imagination and expand your horizons.

When planning your trips, ensure that you remain flexible and adaptable, as unexpected changes or delays may occur due to other planetary aspects. Embrace the opportunities for exploration and embrace the experiences that come your way.

Insight from the stars

Stay grounded, maintain a disciplined approach, and embrace opportunities for growth and self-improvement. By keeping a balanced perspective and being adaptable to changes, you can make the most of the celestial energies and create a fulfilling start to the year.

Best days of the month: January 8th, 9th, 12th, 19th, 20th, 26th, and 28th

February 2024

Horoscope

February 2024 brings a mix of dynamic and transformative energies for Virgo individuals. As the month unfolds, it's important to maintain a balanced approach to various areas of your life. The celestial aspects encourage self-reflection, healing, and growth, urging you to embrace new opportunities and make positive changes.

Love

In the realm of love and relationships, February presents both challenges and opportunities for Virgo. The square aspect between Venus and Chiron on February 5th may bring up past wounds or insecurities, requiring open communication and understanding with your partner. It's essential to approach these situations with empathy and compassion, creating a safe space for healing and growth. The Sun's sextile aspect with Venus and Chiron on the same day offers a chance for deepening emotional connections and strengthening your bond. Use this harmonious energy to express love, appreciation, and support for your loved ones. Single Virgos may also experience positive developments in their love life, attracting meaningful connections and potential partnerships.

Career

Your career takes center stage this month, Virgo. Mercury's sextile aspect with Jupiter on February 19th brings opportunities for growth, expansion, and intellectual pursuits. It's a favorable time for networking, learning, and professional development. Embrace new ideas and approaches that align with your goals. This alignment enhances your communication skills, making it easier to convey your ideas and gain support from colleagues and superiors. However, be cautious of Mercury's square aspect with Uranus on February 16th, as it may bring unexpected changes or disruptions in your professional life. Stay adaptable and flexible, ready to pivot and seize new opportunities that arise. Keep a positive mindset and trust in your abilities to navigate any challenges that come your way.

Finance

February 2024 offers opportunities for financial stability and growth for Virgo individuals. The harmonious aspect between Venus and Uranus on February 7th brings positive changes and unexpected sources of income. This alignment may bring financial windfalls, unexpected job offers, or lucrative investment opportunities. It's a favorable time to take calculated risks and explore new avenues for financial growth. However, be mindful of overspending or impulsive financial decisions. Maintain a balanced approach to your finances, focusing on budgeting, saving, and long-term financial goals. Consider seeking professional advice or guidance to make informed financial decisions and maximize your financial potential.

Health

Health and well-being require your attention in February. The Sun's semi-sextile aspect with Neptune on February 15th encourages holistic healing and self-care practices. This alignment invites you to prioritize self-care, rest, and relaxation. Engage in activities that nourish your mind, body, and spirit. Regular exercise, proper nutrition, and adequate sleep are essential for maintaining your well-being. Additionally, focus on stress management techniques such as meditation, mindfulness, or engaging in creative pursuits. Be aware of Mercury's semi-square aspect with Neptune on February 12th, which may bring some mental fog or confusion. Practice mindfulness and seek clarity to maintain your overall well-being.

Travel

February is a favorable month for travel and exploration. The alignment of Venus with Mars on February 22nd enhances your sense of adventure, creativity, and inspiration. This energy fuels your desire to explore new places, cultures, and experiences. Embrace opportunities to embark on short trips or engage in activities that bring you joy and fulfillment. Allow yourself to step outside of your comfort zone and immerse yourself in new surroundings. However, be mindful of Mercury's square aspect with Uranus on February 16th, which may bring unexpected changes or delays in your travel plans. Stay flexible and adaptable to make the most of your journeys. Consider planning ahead and having contingency plans in place to navigate any unforeseen circumstances.

41 · COMPLETE VIRGO 2024 PERSONAL HOROSCOPE

Insight from the stars

February 2024 holds transformative potential for Virgo individuals. It's a month of healing, growth, and self-reflection. The celestial aspects encourage you to embrace new opportunities, strengthen your relationships, and nurture your well-being. Trust in the process of personal and professional development, knowing that the challenges you encounter are opportunities for growth. Stay adaptable, maintain a balanced approach, and believe in your abilities to navigate any obstacles that come your way. Embrace the transformative energies of this month and allow them to guide you towards a more fulfilling and authentic life path. Remember to listen to your intuition and seek support from loved ones when needed. By aligning with the cosmic energies, you can make significant progress and manifest positive changes in your life.

Best days of the month: February 5th, 7th, 15th, 19th, 22nd, 26th, and 29th

March 2024

Horoscope

March 2024 brings a mix of energetic and transformative energies for Virgo individuals. This month encourages you to embrace change, explore new possibilities, and nurture your personal growth. As the celestial aspects unfold, it's essential to maintain a balance between self-reflection and taking action in various areas of your life.

During this month, you may experience a heightened sense of intuition and spirituality. The sextile aspect between the Sun and Jupiter on March 1st brings opportunities for personal expansion and a deepening connection with your inner wisdom. Embrace spiritual practices, meditation, or contemplation to gain clarity and insight into your life's direction.

Love

In matters of the heart, March brings both challenges and opportunities for Virgo individuals.

The square aspect between Venus and Uranus on March 3rd may introduce unexpected changes or disruptions in your relationships. It's crucial to maintain open communication, flexibility, and adaptability during this time.

However, the harmonious sextile aspect between Venus and Jupiter on March 12th brings the potential for growth and harmony in your love life. This alignment promotes positivity, generosity, and a deeper understanding of your partner. Single Virgos may also attract meaningful connections or experience a renewed sense of self-love and self-worth.

Career

March presents opportunities for career growth and advancement for Virgo individuals. The conjunction between Mercury and Neptune on March 8th enhances your intuition and creative thinking, allowing you to tap into innovative ideas and solutions. Trust your instincts and embrace imaginative approaches in your professional endeavors.

The semi-sextile aspect between Mercury and Saturn on March 16th encourages disciplined and structured thinking. This alignment supports your ability to focus, plan, and execute your goals effectively. Leverage your organizational skills and attention to detail to make significant progress in your career.

Finance

The celestial aspects in March offer stability and potential financial growth for Virgo individuals. The conjunction between Venus and Saturn on March 21st emphasizes practicality, discipline, and responsible financial management. This alignment encourages you to assess your long-term financial goals and make necessary adjustments to secure your financial stability.

The sextile aspect between Venus and Jupiter on March 24th brings favorable opportunities for financial expansion and abundance. It's essential to stay open to new possibilities and remain diligent in your financial planning. Consider seeking expert advice or exploring investment opportunities that align with your long-term goals.

Health

Maintaining your physical and emotional well-being is crucial in March. The conjunction between the Sun and Neptune on March 17th highlights the importance of self-care, rest, and relaxation. Prioritize activities that promote inner balance and serenity, such as meditation, yoga, or spending time in nature.

The semi-square aspect between the Sun and Uranus on March 25th may introduce unexpected energy shifts or disruptions to your well-being. Be adaptable and embrace flexibility in your self-care routine. Focus on maintaining a healthy lifestyle, including regular exercise, balanced nutrition, and quality sleep to support your overall health.

Travel

March offers opportunities for travel and exploration for Virgo individuals. The harmonious sextile aspect between Venus and Uranus on March 28th brings excitement, adventure, and a desire to explore new horizons. Embrace opportunities to travel, whether it's a short weekend getaway or a more extended journey. Allow yourself to step out of your comfort zone and experience the transformative power of new environments.

Insight from the stars

The celestial aspects in March encourage Virgo individuals to embrace change, nurture personal growth, and maintain a balanced approach to various aspects of life. This month provides opportunities for spiritual expansion, harmonious relationships, career advancement, and financial stability. Stay adaptable, trust your intuition, and be open to new experiences. Embrace the transformative energy of March and allow it to guide you towards a brighter future.

Best days of the month: March 3rd, 12th, 16th, 21st, 24th,25th and 28th.

April 2024

Horoscope

April 2024 brings a dynamic and transformative energy for Virgo individuals. This month encourages you to embrace change, assert your individuality, and pursue your passions with confidence. As the celestial aspects unfold, it's essential to maintain a balance between self-expression and practicality in various areas of your life.

During this month, you may experience a heightened sense of assertiveness and determination. The conjunction between the Sun and Chiron on April 8th empowers you to heal past wounds, embrace your authenticity, and express your true self. Use this energy to break free from limiting beliefs and pursue your dreams fearlessly.

Love

In matters of the heart, April brings a mix of passionate and transformative energies for Virgo individuals. The conjunction between Venus and Chiron on April 21st invites you to embrace vulnerability and deepen emotional connections. This alignment supports healing and growth within relationships, fostering greater intimacy and understanding.

The semi-sextile aspect between Venus and Mars on April 27th enhances passion and sparks romantic chemistry. This alignment encourages you to express your desires and needs openly, fostering a deeper connection with your partner. Single Virgos may attract intense and transformative relationships during this time.

Career

April presents opportunities for career advancement and professional growth for Virgo individuals. The sextile aspect between Mars and Jupiter on April 19th brings optimism, enthusiasm, and the potential for significant progress in your professional endeavors. Embrace new challenges and take calculated risks to expand your horizons and achieve your career goals.

The semi-sextile aspect between Mercury and Saturn on April 24th supports disciplined thinking and strategic planning. This alignment encourages you to focus on long-term goals, develop practical strategies, and enhance your organizational skills. Attention to detail and a structured approach will lead to successful outcomes in your career.

Finance

The celestial aspects in April offer stability and potential financial gains for Virgo individuals. The semi-sextile aspect between Venus and Saturn on April 30th emphasizes the importance of responsible financial management. This alignment encourages you to review your budget, prioritize savings, and make sound financial decisions.

The conjunction between Jupiter and Uranus on April 20th brings the potential for unexpected financial opportunities and expansion. Stay open to new possibilities and be willing to take calculated risks in your financial endeavors. Seek advice from trusted professionals to make informed investment decisions.

Health

Maintaining your physical and emotional well-being is crucial in April. The conjunction between Mars and Neptune on April 29th highlights the importance of rest, relaxation, and spiritual nourishment. Balance your physical activities with moments of tranquility and self-reflection to support your overall health.

The semi-sextile aspect between Mercury and Saturn on April 28th reminds you to establish healthy routines and maintain discipline in your self-care practices. Prioritize regular exercise, balanced nutrition, and quality sleep to ensure optimal well-being. Incorporate mindfulness or meditation practices to reduce stress and promote mental clarity.

Travel

April offers opportunities for travel and exploration for Virgo individuals. The semi-sextile aspect between Venus and Uranus on April 22nd ignites your sense of adventure and encourages you to seek new experiences. Embrace travel opportunities that allow you to broaden your horizons and connect with different cultures or perspectives.

The semi-sextile aspect between Venus and Jupiter on April 23rd enhances your enjoyment of travel, bringing forth positive and expansive experiences. Whether it's a weekend getaway or a more extended trip, embrace the transformative power of travel and allow it to inspire personal growth and self-discovery.

COMPLETE VIRGO 2024 PERSONAL HOROSCOPE

Insights from the stars

The celestial aspects in April encourage Virgo individuals to embrace change, assert their individuality, and pursue their passions fearlessly. This month offers opportunities for healing, transformation, and growth in various areas of life. Embrace the dynamic energy and trust in your abilities to manifest positive changes. Align your actions with your values, and you'll experience significant progress and fulfillment.

Best days of the month: April 3rd, 8th, 19th, 21st, 24th, 28th and 30th.

May 2024

Horoscope

In May 2024, Virgo, you can expect a dynamic and transformative month ahead. The planetary aspects will bring both challenges and opportunities, urging you to step out of your comfort zone and embrace growth. Venus square Pluto on May 1st may bring intense emotions and power struggles in your relationships, requiring you to find a balance between asserting your needs and maintaining harmony.

The sextile between Mars and Pluto on May 3rd empowers you to take charge of your ambitions. This aspect encourages you to tap into your inner strength and make significant strides in your career or personal goals. However, the semi-square between the Sun and Neptune on May 3rd warns against falling into illusions or deceitful situations. Stay grounded and trust your intuition.

Love

May 2024 presents a mixed bag of energies when it comes to love and relationships, Virgo. The semi-sextile between the Sun and the True Node on May 5th brings opportunities for soulful connections and deeper understanding with your partner. It's a favorable time to strengthen the bond and work together towards shared aspirations.

However, the conjunction of Mercury and Chiron on May 6th may stir up past wounds and insecurities, leading to communication challenges. It's essential to approach sensitive topics with empathy and honesty, creating a safe space for healing and growth.

Career

In your career, May 2024 brings exciting possibilities for advancement and recognition, Virgo. The Sun's sextile with Saturn on May 7th provides a stable foundation for your professional endeavors. Your hard work and dedication will be noticed, leading to new opportunities and increased responsibilities.

The semi-sextile between Mercury and Uranus on May 9th ignites your innovative thinking and problem-solving abilities. Don't shy away from proposing new ideas or taking calculated risks. Embrace change and adaptability as they will be key factors in your success this month.

Finance

May 2024 brings a focus on financial stability and responsible money management, Virgo. The semi-square between Venus and Neptune on May 10th cautions against impulsive spending or making risky investments. Be cautious and rely on your practicality to make sound financial decisions.

The semi-sextile between Mercury and Jupiter on May 13th favors financial negotiations and collaborations. It's a favorable time to seek advice from experts or explore new investment opportunities. With careful planning and attention to detail, you can secure a stronger financial position.

Health

Your health and well-being require attention and self-care throughout May 2024, Virgo. The conjunction between the Sun and Uranus on May 13th may bring sudden changes or disruptions to your routine. It's important to stay adaptable and maintain a positive mindset to navigate these shifts effectively.

The semi-square between the Sun and Mars on May 20th reminds you to find a balance between your physical and mental well-being. Incorporate stress-relieving activities into your daily routine and prioritize self-care. Listen to your body's needs and make adjustments accordingly.

Travel

May 2024 offers opportunities for exploration and adventure, Virgo. The trine between the Sun and Pluto on May 22nd supports transformative journeys and personal growth through travel. Whether it's a short getaway or a long-distance trip, embrace the experiences that expand your horizons and deepen your understanding of the world.

The conjunction of Venus and Jupiter on May 23rd further enhances the positive energy for travel and exploration. It's an ideal time to plan vacations or indulge in cultural experiences. Embrace the new perspectives and connections that come your way during your travels.

Insight from the stars

The celestial energies in May 2024 encourage you, Virgo, to embrace change, nurture your relationships, and invest in your personal and professional growth.

It's a time of transformation and self-discovery. Trust your instincts and maintain a balance between ambition and self-care. By aligning your actions with your authentic self, you can make significant strides towards your goals and manifest positive change in various aspects of your life.

Best days of the month: May 7th, 11th, 15th, 18th, 23rd, 25th and 30th

June 2024

Horoscope

June 2024 brings a transformative energy for you, Virgo. The celestial aspects of this month encourage you to dive deep within yourself and embrace personal growth. Mars' semi-sextile with Uranus on June 1st ignites a spark of inspiration and encourages you to explore new avenues of self-expression. Embrace your unique ideas and take calculated risks.

The quintile between the Sun and Neptune on June 1st enhances your intuition and creative abilities. You may find solace in artistic pursuits or spiritual practices during this time. Allow your imagination to flow freely and trust the guidance of your inner wisdom.

Love

Love takes center stage in June 2024, Virgo. The quintile between Venus and Neptune on June 2nd opens the doors to romantic enchantment and deep emotional connections. You may find yourself drawn to dreamy and idealistic experiences in love. Embrace the magic but remain grounded in reality.

The conjunction of Mercury and Jupiter on June 4th enhances communication and intellectual compatibility in relationships. It's a time of shared ideas and meaningful conversations with your partner. Explore new depths of understanding and foster a sense of emotional connection.

Career

June 2024 presents opportunities for growth and advancement in your career, Virgo. The trine between Jupiter and Pluto on June 2nd amplifies your ambition and empowers you to make significant strides towards your professional goals. Embrace your leadership abilities and seek ways to expand your influence.

The square between Venus and Saturn on June 8th may bring some challenges and obstacles in the workplace. Patience and perseverance will be key to overcoming these hurdles. Stay focused on your long-term objectives and maintain a diligent work ethic.

Finance

Financial matters require careful attention and planning in June 2024, Virgo. The semi-square between Mercury and the True Node on June 2nd urges you to reassess your financial goals and make necessary adjustments. Seek advice from trusted professionals and develop a practical budget to ensure stability.

The semi-square between Venus and Uranus on June 12th brings unexpected financial opportunities. However, exercise caution and avoid impulsive spending or risky investments. Focus on long-term financial security rather than short-term gains.

Health

Your well-being and self-care take precedence in June 2024, Virgo. The square between the Sun and Saturn on June 9th reminds you to prioritize your physical and mental health. Establish a consistent self-care routine that includes exercise, healthy eating, and stress management techniques.

The semi-square between Mercury and Mars on June 11th may bring temporary physical or mental strain. It's crucial to listen to your body's needs and give yourself ample rest and relaxation. Engage in activities that promote inner peace and rejuvenation.

Travel

June 2024 offers opportunities for meaningful travel experiences, Virgo. The trine between the Sun and Neptune on June 20th enhances your connection to different cultures and spiritual exploration. Consider embarking on a journey that enriches your soul and expands your perspectives.

The semi-sextile between Mercury and Uranus on June 24th sparks a sense of adventure and curiosity. Embrace spontaneity and explore new destinations or embark on weekend getaways. Traveling will not only bring joy but also provide opportunities for personal growth and self-discovery.

Insight from the stars

The celestial energies in June 2024 guide you, Virgo, towards self-reflection, emotional connection, and career advancement. Embrace your intuition and let your creative spirit soar. Stay diligent in managing your finances and prioritize self-care. Through meaningful travel experiences and expanding your horizons, you will discover new aspects of yourself. Trust the transformative energy of this month and be open to the opportunities that come your way.

Best days of the month: June 2nd, 4th, 8th, 12th, 20th , 24th, and 29th.

July 2024

Horoscope

In July 2024, Virgo, the celestial energies bring a combination of transformative experiences and opportunities for personal growth. You are encouraged to delve deep within yourself, confront any unresolved wounds, and embrace self-acceptance. The semi-square between Jupiter and Chiron on July 1st serves as a catalyst for healing and encourages you to address any insecurities or emotional pain that may be holding you back. It's a time for inner reflection and embracing your vulnerabilities as sources of strength.

Love

Love takes center stage in July 2024, Virgo. The square between the Sun and the True Node on July 2nd may bring challenges and conflicts in relationships. It's essential to communicate openly and honestly to maintain harmony.

The trine between Venus and Saturn on July 2nd fosters stability and commitment in partnerships. It's a favorable time for deepening emotional connections and nurturing long-term love. Express your appreciation and devotion to your partner.

Career

July 2024 presents opportunities for professional growth and advancement for Virgo. The opposition between Mercury and Pluto on July 3rd brings a surge of ambition and the desire for power and influence in your career. You may feel compelled to take on new responsibilities and showcase your abilities. This is a time to assert yourself and make a positive impact in your workplace. Embrace your leadership skills and demonstrate your competence and dedication. Networking and building professional relationships will also be beneficial during this period.

Finance

Financial matters require careful attention and planning in July 2024, Virgo. The square between Venus and Chiron on July 6th may bring some financial insecurities or challenges. It's important to trust your instincts and seek practical solutions to maintain financial stability. Review your budget and expenses to identify areas where adjustments can be made. Avoid impulsive spending and focus on long-term financial security. Seek advice from financial professionals if needed and consider exploring new sources of income or investment opportunities. With careful planning and discipline, you can achieve financial stability and growth.

Health

Your well-being and self-care take precedence in July 2024, Virgo. The square between the Sun and Chiron on July 15th serves as a reminder to address any emotional or physical imbalances. Pay attention to your overall health and prioritize self-care practices that nurture your mind, body, and soul. Engage in activities that promote relaxation and stress reduction, such as meditation, yoga, or spending time in nature. It's essential to listen to your body's needs and establish a consistent self-care routine. Prioritize quality sleep, nutritious eating habits, and regular exercise to maintain your vitality and well-being.

Travel

July 2024 offers opportunities for meaningful travel experiences for Virgo. The trine between the Sun and Neptune on July 21st enhances your connection to spiritual exploration and cultural immersion. Consider embarking on a journey that enriches your soul and expands your horizons. Whether it's a pilgrimage to a sacred site, a yoga retreat, or a cultural immersion in a foreign country, seek destinations that inspire your spiritual growth and allow you to connect with different cultures. Embrace the beauty of new places, try new experiences, and engage with locals to fully immerse yourself in the culture and gain a deeper understanding of the world.

Insight from the stars

The celestial energies in July 2024 guide you, Virgo, towards self-healing, commitment in relationships, and professional growth. This is a time for introspection and addressing any emotional wounds that may hinder your progress. Trust your intuition and remain adaptable to the opportunities that come your way. The stars remind you to embrace your personal power and strive for balance in all areas of your life.

By listening to your inner wisdom, you can navigate this month with grace and make significant strides in your personal and professional journey.

Best days of the month: July 2nd, 8th, 15th, 21st, 23rd, 30th and 31st.

August 2024

Horoscope

Dear Virgo, August 2024 brings a mixed bag of celestial energies for you. The planetary aspects indicate a month of opportunities, challenges, and self-reflection. It's a time to evaluate your priorities, make necessary adjustments, and embrace the changes that come your way.

The influence of Mars in Gemini suggests a period of increased mental activity and communication. You may find yourself engaged in stimulating conversations and networking opportunities that can open doors for personal and professional growth. However, be cautious of impulsive decision-making, as the semi-square with Chiron warns against hasty actions.

Love

In matters of the heart, Venus plays a significant role in August. The square with Uranus on the 2nd may bring unexpected romantic encounters or a desire for freedom within relationships. This could create some tension, but it also presents an opportunity for growth and deeper understanding.

For single Virgos, the quintile between Venus and Jupiter on the 6th indicates a favorable period for romance and new connections. Take a leap of faith and explore the possibilities that come your way. For those in committed relationships, the quincunx with Neptune on the 5th and the sesquiquadrate with Chiron on the 11th advise open and honest communication to maintain harmony and address any emotional wounds.

Career

Your career prospects in August look promising, with the Sun's biquintile with Saturn on the 4th enhancing your professional abilities. This aspect provides you with the discipline and focus to excel in your endeavors. Collaborative projects and teamwork are highlighted, as the conjunction between Mercury and Venus on the 7th emphasizes effective communication and cooperation.

However, the quincunx between the Sun and Saturn on the 10th may require you to reassess your long-term goals and make necessary adjustments. It's essential to find a balance between your personal and professional life to avoid burnout. Trust your instincts and make strategic decisions that align with your aspirations.

Finance

Financial matters require careful attention in August, particularly due to the opposition between Venus and Saturn on the 19th. This aspect may bring financial constraints or unexpected expenses, so it's advisable to practice prudent money management. The biquintile between Venus and Chiron on the 19th, however, offers opportunities for financial healing and growth. Consider seeking advice from a trusted financial advisor to make informed decisions.

Health

Your well-being is of utmost importance this month. The sesquiquadrate between the Sun and Neptune on the 6th may bring feelings of fatigue or emotional vulnerability. Prioritize self-care and seek moments of relaxation and rejuvenation. Engaging in activities such as meditation, yoga, or spending time in nature can help restore balance and boost your overall vitality.

The trine between the Sun and Chiron on the 15th offers an opportunity for emotional and physical healing. Use this time to address any underlying health concerns and explore alternative healing modalities if necessary. Remember to maintain a balanced diet, exercise regularly, and get sufficient rest to support your well-being.

Travel

August presents favorable opportunities for travel and exploration, thanks to the quintile between Mars and Neptune on the 6th. Whether it's a short getaway or an extended trip, you'll find inspiration and a sense of adventure. Be open to new experiences and embrace the spontaneity that comes with travel.

Insights from the stars

The celestial energies of August encourage you, dear Virgo, to embrace change, foster communication, and nurture self-care. Although challenges may arise, they present opportunities for growth and transformation. Trust in your abilities, remain adaptable, and maintain a positive mindset. By aligning your actions with your intentions, you can make the most of the cosmic energies and manifest your goals.

71 · COMPLETE VIRGO 2024 PERSONAL HOROSCOPE

Best days of the month: August 7th, 11th, 15th, 19th, 22nd, 23th, and 29th.

September 2024

Horoscope

In September 2024, Virgo, you can expect a month filled with opportunities for personal growth and self-improvement. The planetary aspects indicate a focus on your relationships, both romantic and platonic, as well as your career and financial stability. It's a time to strike a balance between your personal ambitions and your connections with others. With careful planning and attention to detail, you can make significant progress in various areas of your life. However, it's important to remain grounded and realistic, as challenges may arise along the way. Take advantage of the positive aspects to enhance your love life, advance your professional goals, manage your finances wisely, prioritize your well-being, embark on exciting travel adventures, and gain valuable insights from the stars.

The celestial alignments in September bring important messages and guidance for Virgo. The quintile between the Sun and Mars on September 2nd highlights the importance of taking initiative and channeling your energy towards your goals. It's a reminder to trust in your abilities and embrace your assertiveness. The biquintile between Mercury and Pluto on September 12th emphasizes the power of your words and intellect. Use your communication skills to express your thoughts effectively and influence those around you positively. The quintile between Mercury and Mars on September 21st enhances your mental agility and boosts your problem-solving abilities.

Love

In matters of the heart, September brings a harmonious energy for Virgo. The trine between Mercury in Leo and Chiron in Aries on September 2nd signifies an opportunity for healing and growth within your relationships. This aspect encourages open communication and vulnerability, allowing you to address any emotional wounds and strengthen the bonds with your partner. Pay attention to the biquintile between Mercury and Neptune on September 2nd, which enhances your intuition and brings a touch of romance to your interactions. However, the square between Venus in Libra and the True Node in Aries on September 3rd may introduce some challenges, requiring you to find a balance between your own needs and the desires of your partner. Overall,

September offers a favorable period for nurturing love and deepening connections.

Career

Virgos can expect positive developments in their professional lives during September. The Sun's quintile with Mars on September 2nd fuels your ambition and motivation, allowing you to take the lead and make progress towards your career goals. However, the square between Mars in Gemini and Neptune in Pisces on September 3rd reminds you to remain cautious and avoid impulsive decision-making. Collaboration and networking will be beneficial for your career, especially when Venus opposes the True Node on September 3rd, encouraging you to establish meaningful connections that can open doors to new opportunities. Additionally, the biquintile between Mercury and Jupiter on September 10th enhances your communication skills, making it an ideal time to present your ideas and engage in negotiations. Overall, September presents promising prospects for career advancement and professional success.

Finance

Financial matters in September require careful planning and prudent decision-making for Virgo. While the biquintile between Venus and Uranus on September 15th may bring unexpected financial gains, it's crucial to remain cautious and avoid impulsive spending. The opposition between Venus in Libra and Chiron in Aries on September 16th suggests a need to reassess your financial priorities and seek practical solutions to any monetary challenges. Seek advice from trusted professionals and focus on long-term financial stability. The trine between Mercury and Pluto on September 24th enhances your analytical skills, enabling you to make strategic financial decisions. By exercising caution and being mindful of your expenses, you can maintain financial equilibrium and achieve your monetary goals in September.

Health

Your well-being and self-care take center stage in September, Virgo. The sesquiquadrate between the Sun in Virgo and Pluto in Capricorn on September 6th reminds you to balance your personal and professional life to avoid burnout. Take time to assess your physical and emotional needs and make self-care a priority. The opposition between Mercury in Virgo and Neptune in

Pisces on September 25th highlights the importance of maintaining healthy boundaries and avoiding excessive stress. Engage in activities that promote relaxation, such as meditation, yoga, or spending time in nature. Nurturing your mind, body, and soul will contribute to your overall well-being throughout the month.

Travel

September offers opportunities for exciting travel experiences for Virgo. The biquintile between Mercury and Neptune on September 2nd enhances your sense of adventure and intuition, making it an ideal time for spontaneous trips or exploring new destinations. The trine between Venus in Libra and Jupiter in Gemini on September 15th brings a positive energy for travel, indicating that you may encounter new cultures and forge meaningful connections while exploring the world. However, always remain mindful of your safety and adhere to any travel guidelines or restrictions in place. Whether it's a short getaway or an extended journey, travel experiences in September can broaden your horizons and provide valuable insights.

Insight from the stars

Trust your instincts and be proactive in pursuing your objectives. Overall, the stars encourage you to embrace your strengths, communicate with clarity, and take decisive action to manifest your desires.

Best days of the month: September 2nd, 10th,15th,22nd,24th, 26th and 30th.

October 2024

Horoscope

In October 2024, Virgo, the planetary aspects indicate a month of introspection, transformation, and deep emotional exploration. This is a time for delving into the depths of your psyche, uncovering hidden truths, and releasing old patterns that no longer serve you. You may experience intense emotions and inner conflicts, but through self-reflection and healing, you have the opportunity to emerge stronger and more empowered. It's important to create a harmonious balance between your personal and professional life and prioritize self-care to navigate this transformative period. Trust your intuition, embrace change, and allow yourself to evolve and grow. With patience and perseverance, you can make significant progress on your spiritual journey and create a solid foundation for your future.

Love

In matters of the heart, October brings a period of deep introspection and transformation for Virgo. The sesquiquadrate between Mercury in Libra and Uranus in Taurus on October 2nd signifies a need for emotional independence and self-discovery within relationships. This aspect may bring unexpected changes or disruptions, but they serve as catalysts for personal growth. The trine between Venus in Scorpio and Saturn on October 4th brings stability and commitment to your romantic connections, as well as the opportunity for deep emotional bonding. However, the square between Mercury in Scorpio and Mars in Cancer on October 6th may create tension and communication challenges. It's crucial to express your emotions with clarity and empathy. Embrace vulnerability and engage in open and honest conversations to strengthen your relationships. October encourages you to delve into the depths of your heart and nurture authentic connections.

Career

October brings a transformative energy to your professional life, Virgo. The trine between Mercury in Libra and Jupiter in Gemini on October 8th enhances your communication skills, making it an ideal time to present your ideas, negotiate contracts, or engage in networking opportunities. This aspect supports intellectual growth and encourages you to broaden your professional horizons. The opposition between Mercury in Libra and Chiron in Aries on October 8th may bring up past wounds or self-doubt, but it also presents an opportunity for healing and self-empowerment. Embrace your unique skills and talents, and trust in your abilities to overcome any challenges that arise. It's important to maintain a balanced approach to work and avoid overextending yourself. Set healthy boundaries, prioritize self-care, and trust the process of transformation unfolding in your career.

Finance

Financial matters require careful attention and planning in October, Virgo. The sesquiquadrate between Venus in Scorpio and Neptune in Pisces on October 3rd cautions against impulsive spending or making financial decisions based solely on emotions. Take the time to evaluate your financial goals, set a budget, and make informed choices. The trine between Venus and Saturn on October 4th brings stability and practicality to your financial endeavors. It's a favorable time for long-term investments or solidifying your financial foundations. However, the opposition between Venus in Sagittarius and Uranus in Taurus on

October 14th may introduce unexpected financial changes or disruptions. Stay adaptable and flexible in managing your resources. Seek professional advice if needed, and remain mindful of your financial responsibilities. By maintaining a cautious and balanced approach, you can navigate the financial landscape and ensure stability in the long run.

Health

Your physical and emotional well-being take center stage in October, Virgo. The opposition between the Sun in Libra and Uranus in Taurus on October 4th highlights the need for balance and self-care. Embrace practices that promote harmony and stress relief, such as meditation, yoga, or engaging in creative outlets. The square between the Sun and Mars on October 14th may bring a surge of energy, but it's important to channel it wisely to avoid burnout. Take breaks, establish healthy boundaries, and prioritize restorative activities. The sesquiquadrate between Venus in Sagittarius and Mars in Cancer on October 22nd reminds you to nurture your emotional well-being and maintain a healthy work-life balance. Pay attention to your emotional needs and engage in self-care practices that support your overall health. By honoring your mind, body, and soul, you can navigate October with resilience and vitality.

Travel

October presents opportunities for meaningful and transformative travel experiences for Virgo. The biquintile between Mercury and Neptune on October 16th enhances your intuition and creativity, making it an ideal time for spiritual retreats or visiting destinations with a rich cultural and historical significance. Engage in mindful and reflective travel experiences that allow you to connect with your inner self and gain a deeper understanding of the world. The trine between Venus in Sagittarius and Neptune on October 15th further enhances the spiritual and transformative nature of your travels. Embrace the unknown, step out of your comfort zone, and allow yourself to be inspired by the new environments you encounter. Whether it's a solo journey or a group adventure, October offers the potential for profound growth and self-discovery through travel.

Insight from the stars

The celestial alignments in October provide important insights and guidance for Virgo. The opposition between the Sun and Chiron on October 13th brings opportunities for deep healing and self-reflection. It's a time to confront past wounds and work towards personal growth. The trine between Mercury and Saturn on October 22nd enhances your analytical abilities and supports structured thinking. Use this aspect to make strategic decisions and solidify your plans. The biquintile between Venus and Chiron on October 30th encourages you to embrace vulnerability and compassion in your relationships, fostering healing and growth. Trust in the transformative power of the stars and embrace the opportunities for self-discovery and empowerment that October brings.

Best days of the month: October 8th, 13th, 15th, 22nd, 24th, 27th and 31st.

November 2024

Horoscope

In November 2024, Virgo, the planetary aspects indicate a month of introspection, growth, and a focus on relationships. This is a time for deepening connections, exploring your own desires and values, and seeking inner balance. The celestial alignments in November offer important insights and guidance for Virgo. The sesquiquadrate between the Sun and Chiron on November 11th brings opportunities for deep healing and self-reflection. Embrace vulnerability and confront past wounds, allowing for growth and personal transformation. The opposition between Venus and Chiron on November 27th highlights the need for self-compassion and emotional healing within relationships.

The sextile between Jupiter in Gemini and Chiron in Aries on November 2nd brings opportunities for personal and spiritual growth. It's a time to embrace new perspectives and expand your horizons. The trine between Mercury in Scorpio and Mars in Cancer on

November 2nd enhances your communication skills and assertiveness, enabling you to express yourself with clarity and passion. Embrace the transformative energy of November and embrace the opportunities for self-discovery and growth that come your way.

Love

Love takes center stage in November for Virgo, as the planetary aspects bring opportunities for deepening emotional connections and exploring your desires. The opposition between Venus in Sagittarius and Jupiter in Gemini on November 3rd may bring a sense of restlessness or a desire for more freedom within relationships. It's important to communicate your needs and find a healthy balance between independence and commitment. The trine between Venus and Chiron on the same day fosters emotional healing and growth within partnerships. Open and honest communication, along with a willingness to embrace vulnerability, can lead to a deeper level of intimacy. Pay attention to the needs of your partner and engage in activities that nurture your emotional connection. November presents a transformative period for love, where you can experience growth, understanding, and an expansion of your romantic horizons.

Career

November brings a focus on career and professional growth for Virgo. The trine between Mercury in Sagittarius and Mars in Cancer on November 2nd enhances your assertiveness and communication skills, making it an ideal time to express your ideas, negotiate contracts, or take the lead in team projects. This aspect supports intellectual growth and encourages you to take calculated risks. The opposition between Mercury and Jupiter on November 18th expands your horizons and encourages you to explore new avenues of professional development. Embrace learning opportunities and seek out mentors who can guide you on your path. It's important to maintain a balance between ambition and practicality, ensuring that your actions align with your long-term goals. Use this transformative period to set clear objectives and make progress towards achieving them.

Finance

November requires careful financial planning and responsible decision-making for Virgo. The square between Venus in Sagittarius and Neptune in Pisces on November 9th cautions against impulsive spending or making financial decisions based solely on emotions. It's important to assess your financial situation and create a realistic budget. Seek advice from professionals if needed, and consider long-term investments that align with your financial goals. The sextile between Venus and Saturn on November 22nd brings stability and discipline to your financial endeavors. It's a favorable time to review your financial strategies and make adjustments where necessary. Focus on building a solid foundation and managing your resources with prudence. By maintaining a balanced approach and practicing financial mindfulness, you can navigate November with financial stability and security.

Health

Your well-being takes center stage in November, Virgo. The sesquiquadrate between the Sun in Scorpio and Neptune in Pisces on November 4th reminds you to prioritize self-care and establish healthy boundaries. Take time for rest and rejuvenation, engage in activities that nourish your body and mind, and seek emotional support when needed. The trine between the Sun and Saturn on November 4th brings a sense of stability and discipline to your health routines. Establish healthy habits and commit to self-improvement. However, the opposition between the Sun and Uranus on November 16th may introduce unexpected changes or disruptions. Flexibility and adaptability are key to maintaining balance and well-being during this period. Listen to your body's needs, practice mindfulness, and focus on holistic self-care to navigate November with vitality and resilience.

Travel

November offers opportunities for meaningful and transformative travel experiences for Virgo. The biquintile between Mercury and Mars on November 7th enhances your communication and assertiveness, making it an ideal time for business trips, networking, or exploring new destinations. Engage in activities that broaden your horizons and expose you to different cultures and perspectives. The trine between Venus in Capricorn and Saturn on November 22nd brings stability and structure to your travel plans, ensuring smooth logistics and enjoyable experiences. Embrace the transformative potential of travel by stepping out of your comfort zone and immersing yourself in new environments. Whether for work or pleasure, November offers opportunities for personal growth and expanding your horizons through travel.

Insights from the stars

Nurture yourself and communicate your needs openly and honestly with your loved ones. Trust in the transformative power of the stars and embrace the opportunities for self-discovery and empowerment that November brings.

Best days of the month: November 2nd, 4th, 6th, 9th, 17th, 19th and 22nd.

December 2024

Horoscope

December's celestial alignments offer profound insight and guidance for Virgo. The planetary aspects indicate a month of introspection, transformation, and a focus on personal growth. This is a time for deepening your understanding of yourself, releasing old patterns, and embracing new beginnings. The trine between Venus in Capricorn and Uranus in Taurus on December 2nd brings unexpected opportunities for love and personal expression. Embrace change and be open to unconventional connections. The opposition between the Sun in Sagittarius and Jupiter in Gemini on December 7th encourages you to expand your horizons and explore new perspectives while the quintile between Jupiter and the True Node on December 13th highlights the importance of aligning with your life's purpose and embracing your true path. Embrace intellectual growth, engage in learning opportunities, and seek out new experiences. December presents a transformative period for Virgo, where you can undergo profound inner shifts and embrace the potential for personal reinvention.

Love

Love takes on a transformative and dynamic energy in December for Virgo. The trine between Venus in Capricorn and Uranus in Taurus on December 2nd brings excitement and unpredictability to your love life. Embrace spontaneity and be open to new experiences and connections. The conjunction between Venus and Pluto on December 7th intensifies your emotions and brings opportunities for deep emotional healing within relationships. It's important to communicate honestly and authentically with your partner, as this will foster intimacy and understanding. The sextile between Venus and Neptune on December 17th brings a touch of romance and idealism to your love life. Embrace your dreams and fantasies while maintaining a grounded and realistic approach. December offers the potential for transformative experiences in love, where deep emotional connections and personal growth can thrive.

Career

December brings a focus on career growth and professional development for Virgo. The opposition between Mercury in Sagittarius and Jupiter in Gemini on December 4th encourages you to think big and explore new opportunities. Embrace a growth mindset and seek out learning opportunities that expand your knowledge and skills. The square between Mercury and Saturn on December 6th calls for discipline and attention to detail in your work. Focus on organization and efficiency to achieve your goals. The conjunction between the Sun and Mercury on December 5th enhances your communication skills and brings clarity to your professional endeavors. It's a favorable time to express your ideas, collaborate with others, and make progress on projects. Embrace the transformative potential of December and pursue your career goals with determination and focus.

Finance

December requires careful financial planning and a balanced approach to money matters for Virgo. The semi-square between Venus in Aquarius and Saturn on December 5th reminds you to maintain financial discipline and responsibility. Create a realistic budget and avoid impulsive spending. The sextile between Venus and Neptune on December 4th brings opportunities for financial creativity and inspired decision-making. Trust your intuition and seek out investments or ventures that align with your long-term financial goals. However, the square between Venus and Uranus on December 28th may introduce unexpected changes or disruptions to your financial situation. It's important to adapt and make necessary adjustments while remaining focused on your financial stability. By practicing financial mindfulness and maintaining a balanced approach, you can navigate December with financial security and success.

Health

Your well-being takes center stage in December, Virgo. The square between the Sun in Sagittarius and Saturn in Pisces on December 4th reminds you to prioritize self-care and establish healthy boundaries. Take time for rest, rejuvenation, and stress management. The trine between the Sun and Chiron on December 10th brings opportunities for emotional and physical healing. Pay attention to your body's needs and engage in activities that support your overall well-being. The semi-square between Venus and Neptune on December 17th calls for balance and moderation in your approach to health. Embrace a holistic approach to well-being, focusing on nourishing your body, mind, and spirit. By prioritizing self-care and maintaining a balanced lifestyle, you can navigate December with vitality and inner harmony.

Travel

December offers opportunities for meaningful and transformative travel experiences for Virgo. The biquintile between Venus and Jupiter on December 1st enhances your sense of adventure and curiosity. Embrace new destinations and immerse yourself in different cultures and experiences. The semi-sextile between the Sun and Uranus on December 21st brings unexpected travel opportunities or spontaneous trips. Embrace flexibility and be open to last-minute changes in your travel plans. Travel can be a source of inspiration, personal growth, and self-discovery in December. Whether for work or leisure, seize the opportunities to expand your horizons and embrace the transformative power of travel.

Insight from the stars

Trust in the wisdom of the stars and allow their guidance to inspire and empower you. December offers the potential for profound inner shifts and a renewed sense of purpose.

Best days of the month: December 2nd, 7th, 10th, 17th, 21st 23rd, and 29th.

Printed in Great Britain
by Amazon